The story of the Williams sisters is bigger than the bare facts of the tennis record books. They are two girls who came from the ghetto to dominate in a sport that has always been seen as middle class and almost exclusively played by white players. The Williams sisters are proud African-Americans. They celebrate their birthright.

The kids who battered old tennis balls routinely sign deals worth tens of millions of dollars. Yet their triumphs have been forged out of hard labour and tainted by genuine tragedy. Serena and Venus Williams are a phenomenon. They are the very stuff of legend.

INSPIRATIONS SERIES

Series Editor: Rosemary Goring

An easy-to-read series of books
that introduce people of achievement
whose lives are inspirational.

Other titles in the series:

Robert Burns
Bob Dylan
Nelson Mandela

Further titles to follow in 2011

The Williams Sisters

from the ghetto to glory

Hugh MacDonald

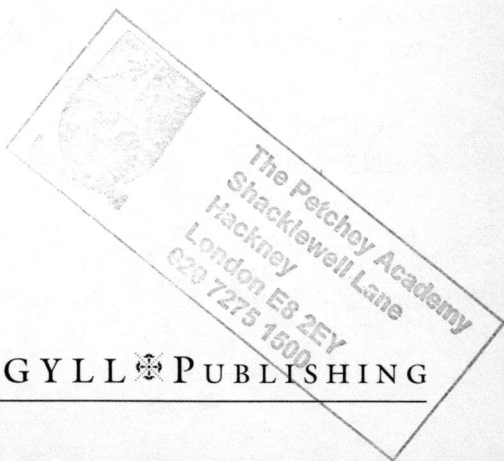

ARGYLL ✤ PUBLISHING

Argyll Publishing
Glendaruel
Argyll PA22 3AE
Scotland
www.argyllpublishing.com

The author has asserted his moral rights.

**British Library Cataloguing-in-Publication
Data.
A catalogue record for this book is available
from the British Library.**

The publisher acknowledges subsidy from the
Scottish Arts Council towards the publication of
this volume.

Scottish
Arts Council

ISBN 978 1 906134 54 9

Printing: JF Print Ltd, Somerset

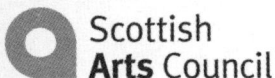

To Catriona and Alastair

Contents

Preface

PAT, PAT, PAT. The ball bounces five times, ten times on the hardcourt surface in Queen's, New York. There is the slightest hesitation by the woman bouncing the ball as a voice of support cries out. Pat, pat, pat, pat, pat. Fifteen bounces, then 20. Serena Williams launches herself into a serving action.

There is a whoosh, a grunt and a crack. Then a shout. The ball is called out. Williams gathers herself. The bouncing restarts. Then, in the flash of a New York milli-second, she throws herself into the air. Her body twists and the ball flies off her racket at 100mph. Her skirt flies up, revealing an acre of purple knicker. There is another call. 'Foot fault.' Fans in the Arthur Ashe stadium let out a communal gasp. Williams is now on the brink of defeat to Kim Clijsters in the semi-finals of the US Open. The call is extraordinary. A foot fault is never called at this juncture of a top match.

Williams seems stunned. She turns for what may be her last serve in the tournament. Then she thinks again, overcome by what she sees as the injustice of the moment. She strides over to the lineswoman. The attitude is aggressive. The racket points straight at the bespectacled official. Serena loses it. 'I swear to God I'll [expletive deleted] take this ball and shove it down your [expletive deleted] throat! Do you hear me? I swear to God. You better be glad – you better be [expletive deleted] glad that I'm not, I swear.'

The chair umpire calls over the line judge to ask what Serena has said. Rules officials are summoned. Serena denies threatening to kill the woman. She is docked a point. The match is lost.

The incident is shocking to witness. I sit high in the media seats watching it unfold. A fury has been unleashed. Immediately, I start scribbling notes. There is the expression of disbelief on the face of Clijsters. The Belgian cannot quite believe she is through to a grand slam final just months after coming out of retirement. Venus Williams, the older sister of Serena, is caught on camera. She is quiet, sombre. Her face betrays no anger, no shock. Serena picks up her bag and strides from the court. It is September 12, 2009. It is the night that Serena Williams exploded.

She later makes a series of apologies as she slowly accepts the full scale of her outburst. At first, she is quietly defiant in the post-match press conference. But her stance softens as the extent of the public relations disaster is revealed to her. She is fined a few thousand dollars, but plays on at Flushing Meadows, winning the doubles with her sister, Venus. But the row rumbles on. Ultimately, the International Tennis Federation's grand slam committee confirms a fine of £53,000. This is a flea bite out of her huge fortune.

But the 28-year-old is also given a three-year suspended ban from the US Open. The penalty kicks in if she commits any major offence before next year. The tennis player from the 'hood of Compton, Los Angeles, is put on probation.

The moment cannot stand alone, however. There is history behind Serena's outburst. There is experience behind the calm demeanour of Venus. The sisters are superstars of tennis. Their fame extends far beyond the sidelines of a court. They are heroines. They are role models. They are also lightning rods for criticism, even abuse.

They are two distinct individuals, but they share a remarkable story. Their road to glory has been charted with statistics. It is strewn with titles. But the story of the Williams sisters is bigger than the dull facts of the record book. They are two girls who came from the ghetto to dominate in a sport that has always been seen as middle class and almost exclusively played by white players. The Williams sisters are proud African-Americans. They celebrate their birthright. They do not hide from a past that includes sharing beds as children.

Serena and Venus Williams, then, are a phenomenon. They are the very stuff of legend. Their story would transfer neatly to a made for TV drama. There would be no need to tweak the script. The truth is dramatic enough. There is the rise from poverty to the unthinkable riches of the top profess- ional players. The kids who battered old tennis balls routinely sign deals worth tens of millions of dollars. There is the controversy over the racism they have faced. Both sisters have been abused on court by spectators. They were at the centre of a demeaning row at Indian Wells, in California, when Venus pulled out of a final against her sister, citing an injury. The mostly white crowd roared in anger. Their father, Richard, said he had been verbally abused. The sisters have never played the tourn- ament again.

Both, too, have redefined the way women's tennis is played. They are strong, athletic and do not take a backward step. The serve of Venus, at 128mph, can outstrip that of Roger Federer, perhaps the greatest male player ever, on the Wimbledon grass. Serena is fearsome as she bullies opponents with an unwavering stare and brutal ground strokes.

But it is off the court that their significance is at its strongest. They are proud to be women. Proud to be black. They make no secret of their faith in God. They are Jehovah's Witnesses. They make no secret of their belief in themselves. They have a self- confidence that shrugs off every setback. They love their sport. But they know that something lies beyond the centre courts. Both Venus and Serena are intelligent women who have continued to seek education while making millions.

They read, they make deals, they design clothes and homes. They win on the court. They learn away from it.

They are not perfect. Serena can be brash, bold and belligerent. Venus can be defensive to the point of rudeness. But a glance at their history shows they may be this way because of what they have had to face. Their success on the court is unprecedented by members of the same family. They have both been ranked the No.1 player in the world. Venus has won five Wimbledon titles, two US Open championships and an Olympic gold medal in 2000. Serena has won three Wimbledon titles, five Australian Opens, one French Open, and three US Opens. The pair have won 11 grand slam doubles titles.

But these triumphs have been forged out of hard labour. They have also been tainted by genuine tragedy. Yetunde, their sister, was shot in Compton, Los Angeles, on September 14, 2003. Yetunde had escaped the danger of the ghetto and moved out to the suburbs. But her boyfriend was from Compton and Yetunde died in a hail of bullets directed at his car. She was 31. She left three children and four grieving sisters.

Venus and Serena seem to have escaped from Compton forever. They live gilded lives of riches and comfort. But they learned lessons in the hard times. The ghetto formed part of their character.

When Serena roars at the US Open, she is protesting against an unfairness she has experienced throughout her life. When Venus looks on, her silence should not be taken as meekness. These are tough, strong women. They have a femininity and an athletic sexiness. But they know what they want. And how to get it. They are the product of two remarkable characters, Richard and Oracene Williams. They are the product, too, of their backgrounds. But they have added their own personalities to the mix. They have never strayed far from the beliefs instilled in them. But they have come a long way from Compton. . .

1. Straight Outta Compton

Believe
A Richard Williams sign that hung
from a court in the 'hood

COMPTON does not 'do' tennis players. Or at least it did not. Compton, a suburb of Los Angeles, is famous for other things. It was an area where many of the locals did drugs. And violence. Some still do.

A city of more than 90,000 souls, Compton was a deadly place as Richard and Oracene Williams planned additions to the family. Gang violence was rife. The Bloods, the Crips, and Mexican gangs all jostled for a slice of the illegal drugs market.

It was the ideal birthplace for gangsta rap groups. The most famous was N.W.A. who released the remarkable album 'Straight Outta Compton' in 1988. But Compton producing a tennis star? That would be like Moscow producing a top-class surfer.

But the Californian city nurtured not one but two of the best women players ever. The crime in Compton has come down since the dreadful days of the 1980s, but the suburb can still be notorious for claiming lives. It is, though, also famous for being the early playground of the Williams sisters.

The story of the sisters is the stuff of legend, even myth. Greatness attracts an extra polish over the years. This story does not need it. The Williams sisters did survive a ghetto upbringing. They did run for cover when shots fired out as they were hitting balls in rundown courts. They knew what it was like to have little except a dream.

The story begins with Richard Williams, the son of a poor sharecropper or farmer from Louisiana, meeting Oracene Price, a nurse in 1970. Oracene had three daughters: Yetunde, Ishea and Lyndrea from a previous relationship. Richard had children who lived with their mother.

Richard and Oracene had two children together: Venus was born on June 17, 1980 in Lynwood, California, and Serena was born September 26, 1981 in Saginaw, Michigan. The family of seven settled in Compton in a small house with the girls all sharing a room.

Richard ran a security firm and worked hard. But he worked even harder on the dream. His company, Samson Security, provided food for the table. His dream dominated most of his thoughts.

That ambition has a hazy beginning. Some say it came when Richard was watching Virginia Ruzici win $100,000 in a tournament. Others say it was Natasha Zvereva winning a championship and the sum was $75,000. But one fact is certain. Richard saw women's tennis paid well. The legend says he turned to Oracene in 1978 and said: 'We got to make more daughters!' Venus and Serena duly came along. The journey from a rundown inner city scheme to the centre courts of the most glamorous cities in the world had begun.

Oracene and Richard picked up every tennis manual and video cassette on the game they could find. They read and watched obsessively. The children were given used and battered tennis balls. They played hand tennis in front of the house at 1117 East Stockton Street in Compton. Then Richard and Oracene took their five daughters out on to courts that were dirty, bumpy and dangerous.

The family would arrive in a beat-up camper van. Oracene and Richard would sweep the court of shattered glass and syringes left by drug users. The children would bound out ready to practise. Then Richard would bring out the equipment.

'It's a radical neighbourhood,' says Richard of his old playground. 'A lot of dope was sold. We played on two courts – that's all there is – they look like trash.' But all that could not stop Richard Williams. Or his children.

Serena remembers: 'Over time Daddy collected all this equipment – ball hoppers, carts, cones, whatever he could find – to make our sessions more like the ones in his books and videos. He really tried to create a professional regime for us on a nothing budget. For a while, the routine was that we had to take out the middle seat of our van so dad could fit the shopping cart he'd somehow managed to acquire, which he would fill with tennis balls and wheel out on to the court.'

Richard believed tennis was a simple sport. He still does. He had the notion that repeated practice and the right mindset would bring results. He watched closely as his children bashed ball after ball after ball.

The older sisters – Yetunde, Ishea and Lyndrea – were good but the younger ones were special. Venus was showing signs of becoming the lithe, powerful athlete the world knows now. Serena had power and attitude.

Daddy pasted up motivational signs all over the court. If you fail to plan, you plan to fail. Believe. You Are a Winner.

The scene was Lynwood Courts. The message was that this was just the beginning for the sisters. Nothing was allowed to distract them from their practice. All remember it as a gruelling but happy time for the family. But this was no jaunt. The Williams family were in the line of fire. Gunshots could be heard all round courts in Compton or Lynwood.

'The shots themselves were not too terrifying until I realised what they were,' recalls Serena. But her father would gently comfort her, advising her: 'Never mind the noise. Just play.'

The sisters had another life, of course. Richard and Oracene believed in education and in God. Good grades were a basic requirement for all the sisters. Attendance at the Kingdom Hall on three nights a week was also compulsory. The family are Jehovah's Witnesses.

But tennis gradually became a huge part of all their lives. Richard suddenly found he had to rearrange his business hours to suit his coaching duties. Oracene changed jobs so she was also on hand to coach and encourage.

Things began to get better. There was the occasional moment of bullying of the children by bystanders as they played what was seen as a rich, white sport. But they could look after themselves. The jibes and the catcalls were all part of growing up in Compton. And doing things that had never been done in the area.

Their equipment began to improve. 'Occasionally, Daddy would add a can or two of new balls and that was a real treat,' says Serena.

Venus was starting to make an impression. She would blast out hundreds of balls over the net. She never seemed to get tired. There was always another ball to hit before she could be persuaded back into the camper to go home.

In 1985 – when Venus was five and Serena was four – the Williams sisters were already causing a ripple in the wider world. One day Venus was watched by grand slam champions John McEnroe and Pete Sampras as she hit balls at a private court in Brentwood, California.

Venus, willowy and small, slammed balls back at an amused McEnroe. The man known as the Brat enjoyed playing with a child who was not in awe of him. Venus was defiant at the other side of the net. 'She told me she thought she could have beaten him,' says Richard.

Other famous stars came along to have a peek at the phenomenon. It was all Venus at that point. Serena still had some growing to do. Serena still speaks of her disappointment at a poor performance when having a hit against Billie-Jean King. On one side of the net, there was a legend. On the other side was a girl of barely primary school age. Yet the pupil was devastated that she did not do better.

When the Williams girls were eight and nine, they traded tennis blows with professionals Zina Garrison and Lori McNeil. They learned how hard the real pros played. The Williams sisters went into the match believing they could win. But Serena had changed. She had been downhearted when playing

Billie-Jean King. She was inspired when squaring up to Garrison and McNeil just a year later.

'We could not hang with them at all, of course, but that was cool,' she says in her biography. 'That was just the silent fuel I'd need to put in the tank to keep me going to the next level.'

It was back to practice sessions with mum and dad. It was back to long days of school and tennis. But the Williams sisters were beginning to believe that tennis was their future. Could two future grand slam champions come straight outta Compton?

Daddy was telling them that they would dominate the sport. And Daddy always seemed to be right.

2. Who's The Daddy

The key to success is looking at something you want and dreaming it's yours.
Richard Williams

HE looks like a fan. The skip cap is pulled down tight against a weak Wimbledon sun. The backpack hangs loosely from an arm. But Richard Williams is a multi-millionaire whose daughters are usually in at the business end at the tennis championships in SW19.

He is standing in his normal prowling area around the media centre. He takes my hand. It disappears into a huge grip. He bends his impressive frame forward as he struggles to understand my Scottish accent. He replies to questions softly in a Southern drawl.

Williams, born in 1942, has mellowed with age. But he was once a man of noise and bombast when faced with the press. Williams always knew he was news. And he helped add a little spice to it.

The son of a poor farmer in Shreveport, Louisiana, Williams has a gift for making unlikely claims. He once said he was going to make a fortune by buying the airspace over India and then charging airlines to use it. He claimed he was going to snap up the Rockefeller Centre in New York for $3.9 billion. He talks almost daily of starting up internet companies. He is always just about to publish a book or make a film.

'You know when you meet somebody and you think he's either insane or a genius?' says Aaron Milchan, a film producer, who has met his share of characters in Hollywood. 'Either he is totally crazy – but that's impossible because there's something totally sane and healthy about his family or he knows something I don't.'

'There's method to his madness,' says Keven Davis, who has advised the Williams family on business and legal matters. 'Don't ever under-estimate Richard.'

No one ever could. Richard made the most absurd statement by saying he could make tennis champions out of two of his children. And he made it come true.

This needs talent, planning and luck. But it demands ambition. Williams is said to have inherited that drive from his mother. 'My mother was my dad, my psychiatrist, my hero, the greatest person who ever lived,' he says.

Serena says: 'My dad always talks about how she helped him be the person that he is. I was pretty young when she passed away, but I remember she was always smiling. He's a very positive person, the type of person who wants to be the best at whatever he does. I imagine her to have been the same way.'

Richard has had to be positive. His beginnings were poor. After leaving school he moved to Chicago for a spell and then on to Los Angeles where he met Oracene. He claims to have slept rough while working in a car wash. He worked hard in his security business in Compton. It was a difficult place to live. It was a harder place to make a legal living.

But Richard survived and then prospered. Like many parents, he saw his future in his kids. That is dangerous for the father and the children. Yet Richard was not the bullying tennis daddy that has scarred the sport down the ages.

'He had a gentle demeanour,' says Serena. 'He was always offering praise and encouragement.' Venus talks, too, of how there were no rows allowed on court during practice.

Richard differs wildly from those tennis dads who were crushed by their drive for success. The most striking example of a dad going too far is Damir Dokic. The Serbian father of Australian tennis player Jelena was jailed in 2009 after making threats against the Australian ambassador in Belgrade. Police said they found seven hunting rifles, a gun and two bombs during the search of his house. This was just the most serious – and bizarre – incident in a history of Damir Dokic mayhem. Other tennis dads have been accused of abusing their daughters both physically and emotionally.

But Richard Williams has brought his daughters up with tenderness. 'There are no bad kids in the world,' he likes to say. 'Just parents who are not worth a nickel.'

He watched many children 'burning out' on the junior circuit. Both Serena and Venus say their dad was interested in their success but dedicated to their happiness.

When he thought Venus was spending too much time hitting a tennis ball, he said: 'Don't get tied up in this or you'll be like the rest of them. You'll be a dummy and a fool.'

This is not to deny his ambition. He was always focused on how to take his girls to the top. He was always sure about how to go about it, too.

Richard wanted to do it his way. The Williams family did not walk the normal path to glory. He had no help from the United States Tennis Association and only briefly allowed the girls to be taught by seasoned coaches.

'I think everyone the USTA helped went down,' he once said. He believes talent can be pushed too hard. It can be crushed by others at a young age. He has a simple formula for improving tennis in Britain and the USA. 'If they're [the tennis authorities] not going to go to the ghetto, and get someone who can play, and who is hungry and willing to play, they're not going to get a champion.' His approach can be summed up in one sentence. 'Attitude is everything,' he says.

He has allowed his children to flourish. Richard does not go to many tournaments now. 'It's my kids' career, not my career. There are so many other things I'm doing.'

Educated at a school called Little Hope, Richard remains a riddle. He says his tall tales are partly to keep people on edge. He likes to watch how his listeners react. Asked about the truth of the claim he was buying the Rockefeller Centre, he says: 'I've never come close to buying it but you should set your goals real high and if you fail, did you really fail at all? If I'm reaching for the stars and all I get is the moon, I don't care. Each year I come out with three businesses. There's some songs that will come out. I'm a singer now also.' He also once said that he had an offer from a nightclub owner for him to sing and Venus to back him on drums.

If all this seems far-fetched, there is an undeniable truth about Richard. His charity work is making a huge difference in California. He has helped under-privileged children find employment and works closely with a cancer charity. Speaking as Venus was about to take part in a final, he once said: 'Sometimes my job gets very sad. If my daughter won this tournament and I didn't look happy it could be because I had lost seven or eight kids while I was gone. About five weeks ago I lost three in one week. So I try to raise a lot of money for them.'

He has been at the centre of the storm as two black women launched their bid for domination in a sport seen as white, middle-class and exclusive. Richard barged his way right into everyone's faces. He would stand in the reserved seats with placards praising his children. He would take on their critics whether in the press or among the fans. He was properly protective of his kids.

But he was never just a tennis dad. Serena talks of how her father once tried to lift every newspaper from the steps of the neighbourhood because a Venus victory had made big news in it. To make everything go a little faster, Richard allowed one of his daughters to guide the van down the street. Unfortunately, the van was guided into a succession of other vehicles. Richard had to go to an ATM and withdraw cash. His attempt at saving a few coins had cost him a wad of dollars.

But he took it all on his substantial chin. He did not blame the daughter. He did not shout or attempt to hit anyone.

After all, it was just another episode in the crazy world of Richard Williams. This was Compton in the 1980s. But there would be many, many more episodes to come.

3. Flourishing in Florida

Is it really worth it to have the fame,
the money and lose your child?

Richard Williams

MOST have a dream. Some achieve it. But how many are ready to walk away from it just when it seems to be in their grasp?

The spectacular progress of Venus meant that the Williams family could leave Compton and poverty behind. Richard, too, was sure that Serena would be a world No.1 some day. Yet he was close to pulling both children out of tennis. Instead, he took the dramatic step of pulling them out of competitive tournaments. He was blunt about his reasons. 'If your child is super good and the child has confidence, your child can be great. The reason I took Venus and Serena out of tennis is because I saw kids from the best neighbourhoods, like Beverly Hills, with broken wrists. I've seen kids get pushed and damaged. You see kids that are told they are nothing. That's past the extreme.'

It was 1991. Venus was ranked No.1 among Southern California girls 12 and under. Serena was ranked best in the under-10 division. The family had now escaped Compton with the help of a sponsorship deal from a sports company. Richard was glad to be away from a violent neighbourhood. 'The problem with living in the ghetto was that on the street we lived on it seemed everyone did drugs. And there was a dead body in the middle of the street every day.'

Life in Haines City, Florida, was different. Coaches had sniffed at the potential of the Williams sisters. They had detected the unmistakable aroma of money. They made their bids to attract the sisters to their academies.

'They showed us pictures of their facilities,' says Serena. 'And there was no denying they were nice. So many courts! So many brand-new tennis balls! So many kids wearing stylish tennis clothes! It would be a whole new environment for us and if you looked up and down their rosters of former students, you could see a number of prominent names on the professional tour, so clearly these people knew their stuff.'

Richard chose Rick Macci, a respected coach, to oversee the development of his children. Richard, of course, still maintained control. 'Richard and I had our ups and downs over a lot of things,' says Macci, 'but he has always been an incredible father to those girls. If he wanted more money, he could have had them playing more. But I remember 50 times when he called off practice because Venus's grades were down. They would be in my office studying French and I'd be saying: "Hey, we've got to work".'

Macci also recalls telling Richard that the girls would have to up their practice. Richard agreed then phoned the next day to say he was taking the girls to Disneyland. It was part of his plan to make sure his daughters had another life. He was beginning to have doubts about professional tennis. As the hype grew and the pressure became a mountain in front of his eyes, Richard considered abandoning the dream. 'When Venus turned 11, I did not want her to play any more. Is it really worth it to have the fame, the money and lose your child? No. I've seen too many parents out there lose their relationship with their kids.'

But the girls were still determined to play on. Venus had always been focused. And Serena found that her desire to win was driving her to extra-ordinary efforts on court. Venus had always been the last one to leave the court when the family trained. Richard remembers that when Venus was just four, 'I must have pitched about 530 balls to her.' He adds: 'That's crazy. You would have to be insane to do that. To a child her age, you should not hit more than 75 balls, or 100 at the most. But every time I tried to stop, she would say: "Just one, one more, one more." I was working with other girls who were older than Venus and they could not hit 500 balls without taking a break. So to see Venus doing it by herself at that age, you just knew she was going to be a champion.'

Serena was different. She loved competition but practice could drain her both physically and mentally. In Compton, she would hit the odd ball over the fence of the courts. She knew that balls were precious and her father would make her go to find it. This gave her a break from the relentless hitting.

But in Florida the practice allowed no relaxation. Macci coached Venus and Serena for four years from 1991 to 1995. 'Six hours a day, six days a week for four years,' says Macci. 'There was not a day that girl did not hit 200 serves,' he adds of Venus. Serena remembers: 'There wasn't a whole lot to do but play tennis, so we played. All the time. Every day after school for about four or five hours. Venus and I were on an accelerated school schedule which meant we were out on court by one in the afternoon. Our teachers overloaded us with homework to make up for the time lost in class.'

At 11 and 9, Venus and Serena were living a hectic life. Their school work and tennis took up the majority of their time. But they also enjoyed karate. And, of course, as Jehovah's Witnesses they attended Kingdom Hall three days a week.

But they were thriving in the Florida sun. Serena remembers how life had suddenly changed. They had been transported to some kind of paradise from the ghetto of Compton.

'Years later my parents told me that Compton itself was part of the problem,' she says of the decision to move the family. 'I did not recognise their concerns at the time but apparently there was a lot of gangland violence and drug use and racial tensions. There were those gunshots ringing out while we played. We were protected from a lot of that as kids because we were always together, always playing tennis.'

She admits that her parents were beginning to worry. 'They did not want us to grow up in such an uncertain environment for any longer than we had to.' The interest and the cash from sponsors meant that a move could be made.

But as Richards watched his daughters develop, he was worried about what was happening around him. He had no concerns about the competition. He was always confident about his daughters' abilities. 'My neighbours accused me of being crazy because before Venus was born I was walking around talking about how she was going to be a champion,' he says. The reality did nothing to disappoint. All the coaches raved over Venus, but Richard began to believe that Serena could be even better.

He was sure he had two future grand slam

champions on his hands. Grand slams are the four major tennis tournaments in the world: Wimbledon, the US Open, the French Open and the Australian Open. Richard was convinced his daughters could eventually win all of them. Yet he was ready for them to stop playing. He had watched the pushy parents and their stressed children on the junior circuit. And he decided it was not for him. Or for Venus and Serena. He pulled them out of all tournaments.

It was a decision that shocked others on the circuit. Junior tennis was considered the only route to the top. Years later, Lindsay Davenport, then world No.1, said she could not believe that the Williams sisters had simply broken through to professional tennis without the lessons that can be learned coming through the ranks. But Richard could not be dissuaded from his decision. The girls continued to practise hard. They did their school work. They lived a family life as normal as it could be with two highly talented sports stars in its midst.

Serena says of her father's decision: 'Daddy just thought we did not need the pressures of the junior tournament circuit and he was right about that. He wanted us to have a normal life. He did not want to be one of those parents pushing and pushing kids down a path they might not necessarily have chosen for themselves. Plus, he thought we would get better competition just hitting with the pros and coaches and working on our fundamentals.'

He was right. Years after the decision, Williams maintained he just did not want to expose his children to 'burn out'. But he was ready to sacrifice his dream for love.

'I wanted to be a dad,' he says. 'Lots of times during interviews, Venus and Serena would say: "Well, my dad, he's my coach." And I would say: "Don't ever say I'm a coach, I'm a dad." I wanted to be a dad more than anything else because you could see the damage that was taking place with some of the kids.'

The kids were lucky, then, to have a father looking out for them. But they had a mother, too. And she is every bit as extraordinary as Richard.

4. Staying Mum

I never had the ghetto frame of mind.
Oracene Price

QUIETNESS is not weakness. While Richard Williams strode through major tennis tournaments proclaiming the greatness of his daughters and the genius of his plans, he had an almost silent partner. At least when it came to speaking publicly. The mother of Venus and Serena has no need for the limelight. She can be spotted in the players' box easily as her hairstyles are big in scope and loud in colour. But she rarely gives interviews. 'I am no celebrity, only my daughters are,' she says. She is, though, strong in mind, strong in faith.

She is Oracene Price. The name tells us everything. When she divorced Richard in 2002, she reverted to her maiden name. She felt no need to be tied to her daughters through name recognition. The bond between Oracene and her daughters is unbreakable. Oracene has delighted in the achievements of all of her daughters. She rejoices in the sporting successes of Venus and Serena. But the achievements of Isha, who is a lawyer, and Lyndrea, a web designer, thrill her too.

'Absolutely my mum believed in me,' says Serena. 'Wholeheartedly. That's a great word about how she felt for her girls. She believed in us all, with all her heart, and she had each of us believing in ourselves and each other. We could do anything we wanted, be anything we wanted, accomplish anything we wanted. She had a great way of isolating each of us and making us feel special.'

But Oracene was destined, too, to grieve for a daughter. Yetunde Price was shot in Compton as she sat in a car on September 14, 2003. She died later in hospital. She was 31. It is believed the intended victim was the driver of the car – Yetunde's boyfriend.

Oracene was devastated. But she went on. She is strong of character. She has had to be. Born in 1952 in Saginaw, Michigan, Oracene was one of a generation of black women who still had to endure the vile racism that gripped America. She experienced the segregation that demanded blacks be educated in separate schools, that demanded seats on the bus were allocated according to the tint of one's skin.

She was part, too, of a black generation who saw the promise of civil rights slowly being realised in the 1960s. She saw Martin Luther King peacefully demand equal rights for blacks. The black leader paid with his life for his drive to improve the existence of the black American. Oracene lived through all this tumult as a young girl and then as a teenager. She tried to grasp the opportunities that Martin Luther King and the civil rights movement had prised from the grip of racists.

The daughter of a car factory worker, Oracene was determined to make something of her life. A graduate of Eastern Michigan with a degree in education, Oracene saw that knowledge could empower. She fell in love, married and had children. This seemed to stall any hopes of a career. Yetunde, Lyndrea and Isha took up all of her time. But tragedy struck when her husband, Yusef Rasheed, died.

Oracene then met Richard. He was taken by her beauty almost immediately. The couple married and moved to Compton where Richard wanted to set up his security business. Oracene was reluctant to go to the Los Angeles suburb. Her life was about improving her circumstances, not going to the ghetto.

'I never had the ghetto frame of mind. When I first moved there I hated it,' she says of Compton. 'Where I was raised we had trees and a house. It was nice. I was ashamed to say I lived in Compton. After a while I got used to it. But my mind was never in Compton. If my daughters said they could not do anything, I'd say "Yes you can. You can do anything you want. Nothing is unattainable".'

She was a willing partner in Richard's plans to introduce all the girls to tennis. Oracene studied the tennis videos and read the coaching manuals. She helped coach the girls while also working as a nurse. Her daughters speak of her serenity and calm. Richard could be wild in his thoughts and ambitions. Oracene was focused, always reminding the children of what mattered.

She believes in education and has a strong faith in God. Both Venus and Serena are Jehovah's Witnesses like their mother and both have been educated. 'I am proud that my daughters are balanced, keep their heads and do not think more of themselves than they should. They know who they are. They are self-confident and proud and they do not try to change to be something they are not,' says Oracene.

Oracene knows what it means to endure hard times. She has lost a husband and a daughter. She is able to put the trivial turbulences of the tennis world into perspective. She has encouraged her daughters to make the most of education. Oracene knows that the tennis will end when both girls are in their thirties.

That is why she joins both Venus and Serena in their charity projects. She also takes an interest in their business ventures. Serena is involved in fashion and acting while Venus has an interior design company. But she is keen to stress that there is more than business and money. 'I always told them you have to stand for something, you have to have some quality in your own life. That's what makes some athletes more substantial than others,' she says.

Oracene may be discreet with the press but she is open in private with her daughters. Serena describes her mother thus: 'Wild and fun and crazy . . . a very strong person, very passionate, very sincere, very honest and spiritual person. The way my mother handles situations, her strength of character, the way she expresses herself has really influenced me. She's a very strong individual.'

Oracene, too, has kept silent about the reasons for her break-up with Richard. She was admitted to hospital in 1999 with three broken ribs, but no charges were ever made against anyone. Asked about Richard in 2007 when she was with Serena on a charity trip to Africa, Oracene said: 'Oops!' She then added: 'I am divorced and for now, I can't tell you much about Richard, the father of my girls. I was very honest with our children that a reconciliation would not happen. They've accepted our divorce and love us, as we both love them. Richard and I will continue to work together for the good of the girls and I truly wish him well.'

If there is any dirty laundry, then Oracene will not wash it in public. She prefers, instead, to give her daughters some stability and discipline. She is aware that they are trailblazers for the black community.

As a Jehovah's Witness, Oracene can play no part in politics. But she says: 'I am neutral when it comes to politics, but I pray for (President Barack) Obama every day, that God will help him in everything he sets out to do. I hope he will make a difference, although he has to be very careful now that he is in a very high office.'

But she prefers to concentrate on the spiritual. 'I'm looking for a revelation to come to me,' she says of her faith. 'It's like anything else you accomplish. You work hard, accomplish it and you're like: What's next? Only God knows what's next. We put God first in our lives and let him guide us. You always plan things but you never know how it is going to turn out. More and more, I believe there is a higher purpose. I am always asking God what it is he is wanting me to do. I don't know myself but I always let God lead me.'

Wherever that may be, her daughters are sure to be not far away.

5. Venus rising, Serena risen

It is my first Wimbledon.
There will be many more.

Venus

THE DECISION had to be made quickly. Was Venus going to be a professional tennis player? She had no doubts. It was 1994, the year of her 14th birthday and she was now eligible to play for money. There were two problems.

First, the rules of the World Tennis Association were changing. If Venus did not turn pro immediately, she would have to wait until she was 16. The tennis authorities were worried about the burnout of players such as Jennifer Capriati and Tracey Austin. They had both burst on to the scene and then suffered. Capriati had a spell in drug rehab and Austin was brought down by injuries to her slight frame.

Second, Richard was still not sure that Venus should play on the circuit. She was ferociously hitting balls with coaches but could she stand up to the strains of the pro tour? The family sat down to have a conference. One Williams legend insists that Richard abstained from casting his vote.

Whatever happened, the result was that Venus would play on tour. 'Venus can be pretty forceful when she sets her mind to it,' says Serena.

On October 31, 1994, a player destined to become one of the all-time greats thus strode out on to court to hit her first ball for money. She defeated Shaun Stafford at the Bank of the West Classic in Oakland. Her win brought her $5,350, which Richard insisted she should keep. He wanted his daughter to have responsibility for her earnings. In the next round Venus faced the top seed in the tournament, Aranxta Sanchez-Vicario who was also the No.2 player in the world. The 14-year-old took the first set and then went 3-0 up in the second. She was three games away from beating a superstar. But she faded. Sanchez-Vicario won the next 12 games and the match.

Venus seemed to take the defeat in her stride. She showed a maturity far beyond her years. Rather than being upset by the loss, she was inspired. Her thinking was simple. If she could come within three games of victory against the world No.2 in her first tournament, then experience would push her to the very top. Her attitude was summed up in the post-match press conference. Asked how the defeat compared with previous losses, Venus replied sweetly that she had never lost a match before.

Serena remembers travelling to the tournament as her sister's hitting partner. 'Venus was really a star by then,' she says. 'She hadn't played a single point as a professional but everyone knew who she was. She'd been written up in all the tennis magazines and in a lot of major newspapers.' The fans liked what they saw. Venus crashed the ball with the force of a man. She was aggressive and feisty. She was an instant success.

The next year Serena decided to follow her sister on to the circuit. Daddy had to be convinced again, but he bowed to family pressure. Serena travelled to a small tournament in Quebec City. It was not to be a debut of promise. She lost 6-1, 6-1 to Anne Miller. 'I think the moment was too big for my 14-year-old self,' says Serena. 'It messed with my head to be playing in front of a great, big crowd underneath these great, big expectations.'

The expectations were rising, too. The world was watching two black sisters from the ghetto make an impact on a sport they associated with Steffi Graf, Lindsay Davenport, Chris Evert. These were all white women who had come from middle-class backgrounds. But the Williams sisters rose quickly. After one tournament, Venus was signed to a $40m deal with Reebok. Serena later made her own deal when she was 16 with Puma. It was worth $15m if she cracked the world's top 20 rankings. Just more than a year later, she did.

All they had to do now was win a title. And they did. Fittingly, their first championship was won together. In 1998, the sisters won the doubles event at a tournament in Oklahoma City. Serena was 16, Venus was 17. The cheque was for $4500. The feeling of victory was priceless. Venus had already endured terrible disappointment in her early career. In her debut at Wimbledon in 1997, she lost to world No.91 Magdalena Gryzbowska of Poland in the first round. Venus had been leading in the second set after winning the first. Again, she faded and lost. But just like the match against Sanchez-Vicario, she was positive about the outcome. 'It is my first Wimbledon. There will be many more,' she calmly told reporters afterwards.

But just months after that defeat to Gryzbowska in SW19, Venus made a huge leap forward. She became the first unseeded finalist in the history of the US Open since it had become a professional tournament. She was crushed by Martina Hingis 6-0, 6-4. But both Williams sisters were on the rise. Venus won her first singles title at the same tournament in Oklahoma where the sisters grabbed the doubles trophy. As early as 1997, Serena had shown her mettle by beating Monica Seles and Mary Pierce, both top ten players, in a tournament in Chicago.

Hammering the ball with previously unseen venom, the sisters soared up the rankings. Richard tried to keep them apart in tournaments. The family hate to see them play against each other. But sometimes it is unavoidable. In the second round of the Australian Open in 1998, the sisters played against each other for the first time in pro tennis. Venus won in straight sets but went out of the tournament in the quarter-finals.

In 1998, Venus won a tournament in Oklahoma on the same day that Serena was triumphant in Rome. They had tournament victories. They had millions of dollars. But they craved a grand slam title. There are only four grand slam tournaments: the Australian Open, the French Open, Wimbledon and the US Open. A player must win one of these before they can have any claims on greatness.

The Williams sisters wanted to be known as the best. They needed major titles as evidence of their brilliance. It was 1999. The millennium was running down. The chances of the Williams sisters winning a major in the 20th century were running out. They contested the final of the Lipton Championships with Venus lifting the trophy. But this cup was not what either sister really wanted. Their first grand slam title came as a doubles partnership in the French Open. They beat Martina Hingis and Anna Kournikova 6-3, 4-6, 6-4. It was sweet.

But history recalls the winners of singles championships. Doubles winners can be lost in the record books. Both Williams sisters looked to the 1999 US Open with excitement. Both felt they could win. One did. On Saturday, September 11, Serena

Williams became the first black woman since Althea Gibson in 1958 to win a grand slam title. At 17, she defeated Martina Hingis 6-3, 7-6.

There was payback in the victory. Hingis had beaten Venus, who suffered from cramps, in the semi-finals of the tournament. 'Venus was so bummed,' Serena said. 'She felt so bad because her legs had totally given out. She was really down, and that encouraged me to be even tougher out there.'

She was more than tough enough. She crushed Hingis with the power of her serve and her all-action game. The moment of victory was greeted by a cry of 'Oh my God' as Serena went down on her knees. Up in the stands, Venus watched her younger sister cavort in a lap of honour around the Arthur Ashe stadium. 'I've never seen her that down before,' Serena said.

Oracene, the mother who oversaw everything on the march to the top, clapped enthusiastically as Serena laughed and cried and waved at the huge crowd. But she is a mother. And she felt for her other daughter. The defeat to Hingis had devastated Venus. 'It was almost like a death, that loss for Venus,' said Oracene. 'She thinks that since she's the oldest sister, she should have been the first [to win a grand slam].'

But as the century ticked to a close, Venus had a further blow. Serena beat her for the first time in a tournament, winning the Grand Slam Cup in

Munich in three sets. Venus had always been the star. Serena had always been the little sister. But in winning a grand slam had Serena done something that her bigger sister would never do? Venus waited just six months into the new millennium before giving her answer.

6. Fusses and feuds

I don't come here to win friends.
I come to win matches.
Venus Williams

THE WILLIAMS sisters were outsiders when they marched through the doors of world tennis as barely teenagers. They still are. They are the biggest names in the women's side of the game. They are surrounded by hype and crowds. But they walk their own road. Both feel no need to make friends in the locker room. This has made them the victim of some petty sniping from other players. The Williams sisters do not seem to care. They fight back when it is needed. They ignore it when it seems beneath them. These are proud women, sure of themselves and convinced of their goals.

They have been involved in various incidents on and off court. They have not been blameless in some of them. But the fusses and feuds have never distracted them from taking care of business. The feuds can be narrowed down to two personalities: Martina Hingis and John McEnroe. Hingis, the Slovak tennis player who won five grand slams and was world No.1 for more than 200 weeks, was an almost inevitable foe for the sisters. She was on top of the world and did not welcome such aggressive opposition as the Williams sisters. Hingis, too, was never slow in filling the notebooks of journalists.

She often upset people. Her opponent in the final of the 1999 Australian Open was Amelie Mauresmo, a lesbian. On the eve of the final, Hingis said: 'She's here with her girlfriend. She's half a man already.' She was irked when comparisons were made between her and Anna Kournikova, the tennis beauty whose looks were never matched by achievements on the court. When asked about the rivalry between her and the Russian, Hingis replied: 'What rivalry? I win all the matches.'

But Hingis was most outspoken on the Williams sisters. She dismissed any claims of racial discrimination against them in an interview in *Time* magazine in 2001. 'Being black only helps them. Many times they get sponsors because they are black. And they have had a lot of advantages because they can always say, "It's racism." They can always come back and say, "Because we are this colour, things happen".'

She said in 1999: 'They always have big mouths. They always talk a lot. It's happened before, so it's gonna happen again. I don't really worry about that.'

The Williams camp has responded in kind. The sisters have been icily dismissive. Venus was asked if she had any bond with Hingis because of their battles on court. 'No. It doesn't mean you like someone more just because you have good matches,' she replied. Serena commented after one Hingis outburst: 'She has little formal education.' Richard, of course, would not shut up. He threw petrol on the flames. 'That Hingis, little miss smarty pants,' he once remarked, 'she thinks she knows all the answers. But she don't know the answers to Venus or Serena.'

He was brutal after Hingis lost to Serena in the 1999 US Open. He said that Hingis looked scared late in the match. This is a controversial remark to make about a grand slam champion.

Hingis replied: 'I wasn't the only person at the end who was scared. She had two match points that she wasn't able to close out. I think she was a bit more scared than I was actually at the end because I've been there, done it. I'm definitely looking for revenge next year.'

Once after being beaten by Venus, Hingis threatened to snap. In the locker room, she headed for the fridge for a drink. Venus was already there and they bumped into each other. Hingis swung her bag at her rival, saying: 'Do you ever get out of the way?'

The Slovak was intensely competitive. All top players are. But she was vocal in the locker room about the threat of the Williams sisters. At the US Open in 2000, she told Lindsay Davenport, the top

US player, to knock out Serena, adding: 'You never win. Beat her.' Davenport, who won a series of grand slam titles, told Hingis she expected her to take out Venus in return. A year earlier, Hingis had told an injured Davenport: 'You gotta hurry back. I can't play the Williamses on my own.'

All this was reported as a pact against the Williams sisters. And it caused an uproar. Venus was typically cool. 'It's like the World Wrestling Federation. You know, tag team.'

Serena was more blunt. 'Obviously no one would want to see an all-Williams final because everyone doesn't like us.'

Oracene was unmoved. 'It is just the black experience,' she said. 'The odds are that someone is going to gang up on you because they are jealous of the press, or whatever it is. That just comes with the territory with us. I take it very seriously because of that. Because of who Venus and Serena are, even the worst girl in the world would get up to play them more than they would to play their counterparts. I prepared them for this.'

The Williams sisters stayed aloof in the locker room and aggressive on court. Arantxa Sanchez-Vicario said after Serena had rifled a ball at her head: 'They have no respect.' Lisa Raymond, a player on tour, added: 'I do not know why they have to be so unpleasant. Lindsay Davenport has won grand slams and still manages to be cordial to the other players. They should be able at least to say "hi" in the locker room.'

The US Open was also the scene of an infamous incident. In 1997, Irina Spirlea of Romania was involved in a tense duel with Venus. At a changeover of ends in the second set, the Romanian seemed to change direction to bump deliberately into Venus. Spirlea then sat down, looked to her friend in the stands and smiled. Was she trying to bully Venus? If so, it did not work. Venus won in three sets.

But the unpleasantness continued after the match. Richard accused Spirlea of racism, adding that she was an 'ugly, white turkey'. Spirlea hit back in her press conference. She said Venus was arrogant. 'I'm not going to move. She never tries to turn. She thinks she's *the* [expletive deleted] Venus Williams.'

Venus played down the incident immediately after the match. She said: 'I thought we both weren't looking. I'm sorry she feels that way. It's not a big thing to me. No one said: Excuse me.' Later she said: 'I was locked in an epic battle, and I had no idea what I was doing, and she was playing unbelievable. It just happened. She got blamed because of the way she acted later, and then she laughed after, but I didn't have time for laughs and games because I wanted to reach the final. I went over and started to read my notes. People blamed her for the bump, but I guess I didn't move. Everybody got a kick out of it, I guess.'

John McEnroe also had the sisters in his sights. The New Yorker is the voice of American tennis. He commentates on all the major matches for television. With a career as a legendary player behind him, he is never shy at giving opinions. These have rankled with the Williams sisters. He once told The New Yorker magazine: 'Any good male college player could beat the Williams sisters.' But he was also outspoken about their behaviour off court. 'They are all as cold as ice,' he said. 'Nor do I particularly want to have anything to do with them until they start to show people in the sport a little more respect.' He added, somewhat unnecessarily: 'I can't say that I'm getting on with them that well.'

He reserved his toughest words for Serena. He believed that she was spending too much time on her acting career and on designing clothes. 'It's a shame that Serena's priority seems to have been to design clothes and act rather than play tennis. But I think she'll realise that she's never going to be the new Meryl Streep,' he said.

There is no sign that these little storms have pushed the Williams sisters off course. Hingis has left tennis, serving a ban for drug use which she denies. McEnroe remains on the sidelines, ignored by the family. Spirlea is retired and Venus went all the way to the final after the bumping incident.

The feuds and fusses have supplied gossip and some entertainment. But the real action has been on the court. . .

The Williams Sisters

7. Decade of Dominance

This was meant to be.
Venus after winning Wimbledon
for the first time

THE MILLENNIUM dawned bright and hopeful for Serena. She had her grand slam singles titles in the bag. Venus, though, was down. She had suffered from tendinitis. There were rumours that she was going to quit tennis. Richard, almost inevitably, stoked the speculation. 'I would like to see her retire now. I would love to see her do that.' Was he kidding? Or was he preparing the tennis world for a shock announcement?

The gossip stopped when Venus returned after five months away from the game to play at the Betty Barclay Cup. It was replaced by the thunder of publicity as Venus won Wimbledon in June 2000. It was a stunning victory. She became the first black champion at Wimbledon since Althea Gibson in 1957 by destroying Lindsay Davenport 6-3, 7-6. Venus beat Serena in the semi-finals and the younger sister reportedly cried for half an hour in the locker room. For Venus, though, the final was the moment she had waited for all her life.

'I always expected to win grand slams. This was meant to be,' she said after climbing into the stands and hugging her sister. 'It's really great because I've worked so hard all my life to be here,' said Venus. 'It's strange. I always dream I win a grand slam. When I wake up, it's a nightmare. Now that I've got it, I don't have to wake up like that any more.'

Venus had been electric on the Centre Court. She moved like an angel. She hit like a boxer. Her strength and athleticism reduced Davenport to a helpless bystander. But she was gracious in defeat. 'You knew eventually she was going to win a grand slam,' Davenport said. 'It's nice to see the monkey get off her back. Both Serena and Venus are going to win more grand slam titles. Venus is going to be a lot tougher to beat now that she has this first one under her belt.'

This was not a reckless prediction. But Davenport could not know how the Williams sisters would dominate the sport. From 2000 to 2009, they won just about half the singles grand slam titles available. This is an astonishing feat. They also won Olympic gold medals and doubles grand slam titles. Both were hampered by injury. But both came back to win at the very top. Both were struck by grief at the death of their sister in a drive-by shooting. But both came back to win. The sisters lead the all-time money list for women tennis players with $28m and $25m for Serena and Venus respectively. But both continue to compete.

Venus's Wimbledon victory seemed to have burst the dam. Grand slam titles flowed. So far, she has won seven: Wimbledon 2000, 2001, 2005, 2007, 2008. Serena has won 12 grand slam titles: Australian Open 2003, 2005, 2007, 2009, 2010, French Open 2002, Wimbledon 2002, 2003, 2009, US Open 1999, 2002, 2008. Over 2002 and into 2003, she had the Serena Slam. That is, she held all four major titles at the same time, if not in the same season.

But 2000 was the year of Venus. The Wimbledon victory was immediately followed by a triumph in the US Open. It was extra special. Venus played unstoppable tennis as Davenport was again defeated in straight sets. The next month Venus won the gold at the Sydney Olympics beating Elena Dementieva 6-2, 6-4 and then took the doubles gold with her sister as they thrashed Miriam Oremans and Kristie Boogert 6-1, 6-1. The year had been fantastic. Venus believed her career could only get better. And it did. Wimbledon was won in 2001 with Justine Henin becoming the victim of Venus in the final. 'This year was a lot more difficult to win,' said Williams, 'I thought a lot more.'

The season suddenly became unbelievable. Back in their homeland, the sisters reached the final of the US Open. More than 20 million Americans watched on television. Venus won in straight sets in the first grand slam final between two sisters for 117 years. Serena said: 'I'm disappointed but only a little because Venus won.' The older sister said: 'We worked hard and we believe in ourselves. Then we kind of stepped up and made it happen.'

The sisters then seemed to make the grand slam titles a family business. Venus took pictures of Serena as she celebrated her win in the French Open of 2002. Venus was defeated but was delighted for Serena. 'Hopefully, we can build a rivalry and we'll be able to do this a lot,' said Serena. 'Make a legacy, then retire champions.'

Then there was the big one. The sisters met in a Wimbledon final for the first time. On July 6, 2002, the Centre Court erupted as Serena won her first title at the All England Club defeating Venus 7-6, 6-3. Richard was not there. He could not bear to watch and flew home before the final.

Serena then won her third straight grand slam title by beating Venus again at the US Open. 'I wanted to win so bad,' said Serena. She was not finished. She completed the Serena Slam by beating Venus in three sets at the Australian Open in January 2003. Serena held all the major championships.

Serena, though, later dubbed it the So-and-So Slam. She named it after a boyfriend who cruelly dumped her. The American football player had dated Serena but suddenly went quiet on her. 'This guy tore my heart in half,' she says. 'Then he ripped up those pieces and stepped on them and backed his car over them.' She vowed: 'Tennis will see me through.' And it did. She looks back on the break-up with wisdom and humour, but states that it also gave her the motivation to prove something 'to the guy and to myself'.

Serena proved she was one of the best players who has ever lived. And Venus has shown that she is a champion, particularly at Wimbledon. The decade of domination was to be ended with two consecutive Wimbledon finals between the pair. Venus won her fifth Wimbledon title in 2008, beating Serena 7-5, 6-4. 'It's unbelievable that I have won five, especially with some of the injuries that I've had. To know every time I come back I have the chance to make history. . . I love this place,' she said.

It was 2009 and it left Venus needing only one more Wimbledon singles title to match Billie-Jean King's tally of six, with only Steffi Graf (7) and Martina Navratilova (9) ahead of that among modern players. It was Venus's first win over Serena in a grand slam final since the 2001 US Open. It was also a smashing match. There have been accus-ations that the sisters do not play all-out against each other. But the intensity of the grand slam finals disproves this theory.

And they came back to do it all over again in 2009. This time it was the turn of Serena to win the battle of the sisters. Venus, with her leg heavily strapped, was defeated 7-6, 6-2 by her younger sister. But in the semi-final Serena had been one point away from going out of the tournament. She survived match point against Elena Dementieva.

'The match is never over until you shake the opponent's hand. It's like you never give up and you always keep fighting. It's just a good lesson for life, not even just in sports, but in life as well. I usually go kamikaze when I'm down. So if I'm going to go out, I'm going out like a hero or something. Nothing to lose. That's kind of how I felt. I just think almost every grand slam I've won I've been down match point in a match before, a lot of them. No fewer than at least two Australians. Definitely here at Wimbledon.'

She said of the final victory over Venus: 'This is one of the few times I didn't expect to come out with the win today. I felt like I had nothing to lose. I felt like all I had to do is go out there and do my best, just stay even, because she's such a good player.

'When I won that first set, I was like, wow, this is great. No matter what, I'm a set away. So I was just trying to relax. I really wanted to stay calm because I felt like I was getting closer to the goal. Sometimes if I get too pumped or if I grunt too loud, I lose. I just want to stay relaxed, stay calm and stay focused more than anything.'

Serena's victory brought her within one of Billie-

Jean King's grand slam singles titles total but she said: 'I'm really just playing for me, whether I'm the greatest or not. I can't even put myself in a sentence with the greatest, because I think of people like Martina Navratilova and Steffi Graf and Billie-Jean King. They were such great champions. To even be mentioned with those people is a real honour to me. I feel like I'm really young. I feel like I'm only thinking about my career and continuing playing.'

Ten years on from her first grand slam title, Serena had done it again. The decade of dominance had been sealed at the home of tennis.

8. The Battle of Indian Wells

The ugliness was raining down on me.
Serena Williams

DOMINANCE on court marked the decade for the Williams sisters. That is the positive side of ten years of hard work in the game. But both will never forget the night of March 15, 2001, in West California. The tournament was the Pacific Life Open. It erupted in boos, abuse and rows over racism. It left a mark on both sisters.

The build-up to the explosion of controversy was simple, even straightforward. The Williams sisters had avoided playing in the same tournaments, except for the grand slams, of course. But Indian Wells was, and is, a big, prestigious competition. The sisters were scheduled to meet in the semi-finals. And this duly came to pass. At least, they both qualified to play in the semi-finals. The television networks anticipated huge viewing figures. The court was packed with 16,000 spectators. Venus and Serena seemed ready to walk out on court. Pam Shriver, a tennis commentator, remembers: 'I got word in my earpiece 20 seconds before we were going on air. Venus is not playing tonight. She is pulling out with right knee tendinitis.'

The response was dramatic. The crowd booed. Some went to get their money back. Venus said when asked about the refunds: 'I don't have any money to give them back.' Refunds were given. But the Williams sisters were embroiled in a nasty row. Part of the anger was because Venus and Serena sometimes pulled out of tournaments because of injury. This was seen as part of the Williams agenda just to concentrate on the grand slams. Other fans at Indian Wells believed Richard had told Venus that she was injured so the sisters would not have to play each other. This was fuelled by Elena Dementieva's news conference after her defeat to Venus in the tournament. Asked to predict the outcome of the match between the sisters, she replied: 'I don't know what Richard thinks about it. I think he will decide who's going to win tomorrow.'

There were accusations that all matches between the Williams sisters were fixed in advance with Daddy telling which sister to win. There has never been any evidence of this collusion. And their clashes have been full of good quality tennis all served up with their customary feistiness.

'The whispered charges against us didn't really deserve an answer, but there they were,' said Serena. 'The tournament directors didn't really do anything to discourage people from this view.' But all the spectators were furious about the lateness of the announcement that Venus would not play. The fans were left staring at an empty court.

The Women's Tennis Association insisted they had no prior knowledge that Venus was going to pull out. The Williams camp tells a different story. Serena was on great form, beating Lindsay Davenport in straight sets in the quarter-finals. But Venus was struggling. She had beaten Dementieva but heat exhaustion had led to cramps during the match. Her knee was also injured.

The Williams insist that on the day of the semi-final Venus told the tour trainer that she could not play. She had slept overnight, hoping that the pain would go away. It did not. What happened next is lost in the fog of different reports.

The Williams camp says that Venus was insistent. She knew the three grand slams of French Open, Wimbledon and the US Open had still to come that year. The Indian Wells tournament was important. But not important enough to endanger the rest of the season. The Williams camp said the tournament trainer would not give her permission to pull out, hoping the pressure would build on Venus and she would be forced to play. She did not.

The announcement was greeted with uproar. Venus was blamed for not telling everyone sooner. Bud Collins, the leading US tennis writer, said at the time: 'If she was hurting, she should have let them know in the morning. And I thought she should have gone on court to say sorry.' Venus insists she did tell the authorities in the morning. She adds that she told them again two hours before play was scheduled to start. But going on court to make a personal apology might have been a good idea.

The crowd left the tournament in an angry mood. Many came back the next day for the final. Serena was to play Kim Clijsters, the talented Belgian player. It was contested in an atmosphere as ugly as anything witnessed on a tennis court. One clash was missed by most in the stadium but was reported in giant headlines later. Richard said he had been abused with the n-word. He claimed it was used several times by people in the crowd and one man reportedly said: 'I wish it was '75. We would skin you alive.'

Richard walked to his seat with Venus to the accompaniment of boos. Serena stepped on to the court before Clijsters and there was pandemonium. 'They were loud, mean, aggressive,' she said of the crowd. 'The ugliness was raining down on me. I didn't know what to do. Nothing like this had ever happened to me.'

Serena was shaken to the tips of her sneakers. 'It was like some genteel lynch mob,' she said of the sight of the mostly white crowd venting their anger. 'I do not mean to use such inflammatory language to describe the scene, but that's really how it seemed from where I was down in the court.'

Serena also claimed she heard the n-word 'a couple of times'. The crowd loudly and consistently cheered for Clijsters. A Belgian woman was being supported in preference to an American women in a tournament held in the heartland of US tennis. Serena missed a first serve and it was greeted with joy. A double fault was met with cheering. There was silence when she won a point. But she hung in. 'I was just a kid and they were ripping me,' she said, looking back in her autobiography. 'I was just a teenager. How can you justify treating a child so badly?'

But Serena is a champion. She used the catcalls to motivate her. She prayed. She ran. She fought for every point. She won 4-6, 6-4, 6-2. She was gloriously dignified in victory. On court, she told an interviewer that she wanted to thank her dad, Venus, and the few people who cheered for her. And she added: 'To those of you who didn't, I love you anyway.'

The match was over but the row rumbled on.

Serena was asked if race had anything to do with the abuse she endured. 'Race? I think, you know, black people have been out of slavery now for just over a hundred years, and people are still kind of struggling a little bit. It hasn't been that long. I don't know if race has anything to do with this particular situation. But in general I think, yeah, there's still a little problem with racism in America.' Venus, ten years later, was cautious in all her responses. But she insisted she had heard racial epithets.

The controversy has polluted the decade since for women's tennis. The Williams sisters feel they were racially abused and that their situation was not handled with any sensitivity by the tennis authorities. Should Dementieva have been censured for her comments about match-fixing? Should the tournament trainer have been questioned about just when he was told Venus could not play? Should the abuse have been investigated and attempts made to trace the perpetrators? The answer is surely 'yes' to all these questions. Yet no formal investigation was launched and Dementieva was not fined.

The Williams family drove away from Indian Wells in 1991 in a sombre mood. 'It was the strangest, most unsettling ride,' said Serena, 'because usually after a big tournament win we would all be giddy and excited. But here it was like we had been stunned into silence. We all knew what we had seen and experienced and it just hung there in the car with us like a pall.'

In the immediate aftermath of the tournament, Serena was asked if she would return to Indian Wells to play. 'I have a championship to defend next year. You'll probably see me here,' she said. The

Williams family have never travelled to Indian Wells on playing duty since. The boycott could be punished by fines from the Women's Tour Association who have the power to insist the top players contest the big tournaments. But there have been no sanctions against the Williams sisters. 'I don't care if they fine me a million dollars,' said Serena, when the hurt had fully set in. 'I will not play there again.' And neither will Venus.

The Williams Sisters

9. Althea, Arthur and Jim Crow

What infuriated me most was having a white Richmond type come up to me somewhere in the world and say I saw you play at Byrd Park [in Richmond] when you were a kid. Nobody saw me play at Byrd Park, because when I was a kid it was for whites only.

Arthur Ashe

IN THE MOMENT of their greatest victories, Venus and Serena were keen to pay tribute to those who had gone before them. They needed to acknowledge the black players who had defied the odds to win grand slam tournaments. The name of Althea Gibson, the black player who won three grand slam tournaments, was first on Serena's lips when she won the US Open in 1999. Gibson had been the last black woman to have a grand slam title. She won the French Open in 1956, and Wimbledon in 1957 and 1958.

Serena had updated the history of black tennis by winning at Flushing Meadows. 'It's really amazing for me to even have an opportunity to be compared to a player as great as Althea Gibson. One of her best friends told me she wanted to see another

African American win a slam before her time is up. I'm so excited I had a chance to accomplish that while she's still alive.'

Serena, of course, won the tournament in Arthur Ashe Stadium, named after the 1968 US Open champion and the last black American to win a major – Wimbledon – in 1975.

At Wimbledon in 2000, Venus won her first grand slam tournament, beating Lindsay Davenport. Venus, too, immediately said she was honoured to follow in Gibson's footsteps, adding: 'I know she's somewhere watching this. She was watching when Serena won the Open.' And when Serena was enduring the boos of Indian Wells, she invoked the spirit of Gibson. 'I kept thinking of Althea Gibson and how she had to deal with some of the vitriol. I remember reading that Althea had to sleep in her car when she was out on the road travelling to all these tournaments because she could not stay in the hotels.'

To understand Serena and Venus, one has to look at the experience of Ashe and Gibson. And to appreciate the struggles of Ashe and Gibson, one has to be introduced to an evil presence named Jim Crow. The origin of the phrase Jim Crow is not known with certainty. Most agree it came from a song, Jump Jim Crow, which mocked African Americans and was performed by white actor Thomas D. Rice who had his face blackened by make-up. Jim Crow laws were an evil perpetrated on African Americans for almost a century.

The slave was supposed to be freed by the Civil War of the 1860s. He and she were, though, subject to laws that restricted their freedom. The Jim Crow laws were enacted between 1876 and 1965. They ordered racial segregation in all public facilities. There were schools for blacks and schools, mostly with better facilities, for whites. There were separate toilets for the races. Blacks had to sit at the back of the public bus. Shamefully, some of these laws survived until modern times when the Supreme Court ruled them out. Althea Gibson had to play through these severely racist times. Arthur Ashe was brought up in them.

Gibson was an extraordinary force. She came from Harlem, a black ghetto, and triumphed at Wimbledon in the 1950s, where the atmosphere was white and rich. Gibson was born in poverty and died after declaring herself broke. She took her first breaths in Silver, South Carolina. She was the daughter of sharecroppers (poor farmers) who moved north when Althea was just three to find work in hard times. Althea's father became a mechanic in New York. The five children of the Gibson family lived a basic life in the teeming streets of Harlem. But Althea was tough. She defended her brothers and sisters from bullies. 'No one dared pick on us,' said one of her brothers. 'Althea would beat up on anyone.'

She found tennis in the strangest way. It was on her doorstep. One morning she came down on to the street to find two bats and a sponge ball. She and a friend began playing immediately. Althea, who had been trained as a boxer to tame her unruly spirit, took to the game immediately. But there were few places for her to play. She could have a game at the black tennis club in Harlem and she was able to play in black leagues. But Althea wanted desperately to be part of the United States Lawn Tennis association events. If she could not play in them, she could not play in a grand slam tournament.

The doors took a long time to open for Althea. She needed strong support from black business-men and politicians. But eventually she was allowed into the US Open in 1950. She went on to win three grand slam tournaments, including two Wimble-dons. The sight of a strong, black woman winning the title in 1957 is said to have shocked the Wimbledon crowd into a strained silence.

But if Althea had the rags in Harlem, she found the riches hard to come by. Tennis was an amateur sport then and she struggled to make a living. She gave up tennis to play on the professional women's golf tour and also starred in a film with John Wayne. But she remained poor in her old age. She said of tennis: 'After years of it, I am still a poor Negress, as poor as when I was picked off the base streets of Harlem and given a chance to work my way up to stardom. I am much richer in knowledge and experience. But I have no money.'

In 1995 it was reported in a tennis magazine that Gibson was destitute. Almost $1m was donated to the champion by the public and players after an appeal was launched. Later that year she had a stroke. She died in 2003 in New Jersey.

The story of Arthur Ashe is dramatic and, finally, as heartbreaking. He was brought up in Richmond, Virginia, where the Jim Crow laws were strong. He could not play against the white boys in his area and had to travel to St Louis for a game. His mother died when he was six and Arthur always carried an air of sadness as well as dignity. It did not stop him from leading a life of purpose.

He graduated from high school and earned a tennis scholarship to UCLA, the equivalent of a top university in British terms. He thrived in sport but he also showed that he was clever and willing to work. He won the national college championship in 1965 but also graduated in 1966 with a BA in Business Administration.

He served in the army, becoming a lieutenant, and then made good use of the tennis talent that he had developed on the public courts near his home. He became the first African American man to win grand slam tournaments. But his triumphs on court are just part of his story.

Ashe was much more than just a sportsman. He organised the Association of Tennis Professionals to improve the conditions of all players as top-class tennis abandoned amateurism to become a professional sport. He protested loudly against apartheid in South Africa. This was an evil system that decreed that people of colour should not have the same rights as white people. Arthur travelled to South Africa to make his views known and he was arrested in 1983 when protesting over apartheid at the South African Embassy in Washington. In 1992, he was again arrested in Washington when objecting to the treatment of Haitian immigrants to America.

But Arthur Ashe suddenly encountered health problems. A seemingly healthy young athlete, he suffered a heart attack in 1979 that required surgery. He required another operation in 1983. His condition forced him to give up tennis but it had a terrible, additional after-effect. It was revealed in 1992 that the blood transfusions given to Arthur had infected him with HIV. He formed the Arthur Ashe Foundation for Aids. He never gave up hope over fighting the illness. He worked right up to the end of his life to help fellow sufferers. He died in 1993. He was just 49. He had become a national hero beyond tennis.

The sport paid its dues of respect by naming the centre court at Flushing Meadows, where the US Open finals are played, after him. The best of the personal tributes was probably made by Andrew Young, former US delegate to the United Nations, who said of Arthur: 'He took the burden of race and wore it as a cloak of dignity.'

But Ashe probably summed up his life and beliefs best when he wrote: 'If I were to say, "God, why me?" about the bad things, then I should have said, "God, why me?" about the good things that happened in my life.'

Arthur Ashe and Althea Gibson stand proudly in the best traditions of tennis. But they were trail-blazers, too, for a couple of kids from Compton.

10. Sister Act

Long before fans and reporters knew us, our parents taught us that our relationship is much more important than being successful in tennis or getting ahead in the world.

Venus on Serena

THE BEDROOM in Compton was cramped. The noise outside could be loud, even scary. Inside, there was regularly a whispered conversation.

Serena: 'Don't go to sleep before me.'

Venus: 'I am tired, Serena.'

Serena: 'Well, I'm scared.'

There is one year, three months and nine days between Venus and Serena. They have grown to be the best women tennis players in the world. But Venus will always be big sister.

'Venus was my protector. I'm not quite sure how the others saw her but to me she was like a benevolent bodyguard, on the constant lookout for anything that might cause me trouble or distress,' says Serena. The five sisters shared one bedroom with two sets of bunk beds in Compton. Serena had to sleep with one of her sisters. She always chose Venus. There was a bond between them almost immediately. Yetunde, Isha and Lyndrea always said that Venus and Serena were brought up slightly differently. They felt their parents had mellowed. They were less strict on the youngest two.

It was a family who prayed together and played together. The visits to the public tennis courts in the beat-up camper were part of their tennis education. But the sisters also played outside their home in Compton. There was hand tennis. And Serena and Venus even threw dirt on the ground to make believe they were playing on the ash of Roland Garros, the home of the French Open.

Family life could be chaotic, too. Five sisters in one bedroom amounted to a lot of work. Serena played on the fact that she was the youngest. Venus always helped her clear up the mess and sort out her clothes. 'Venus never seemed to mind,' says Serena. The sisters enjoyed their schooldays. Both are intelligent. Both always wanted to do well in anything they were involved in.

But Serena sometimes needed to be looked after. Once when she forgot her dinner money, Venus gave her sister the money from her pocket. It was just one incident of many. Venus knew she was the big sister. She knew that post came with responsibilities. Venus even allowed Serena to cheat on court when they were young. Serena was desperate to win and could not compete against the power and ability of her big sister. Serena admits she called some balls out that were in. But Venus just smiled. 'And she won, too,' says Serena.

The sisters were destined to play against each other in serious competition. It happened sooner than Richard had believed would be the case. Serena sneaked into her first competition and came up against Venus in the final. The result was inevitable. Venus won easily in straight sets.

Serena recalls: 'At the awards ceremony they gave Venus a nice gold trophy. They gave me a nice silver one as the runner-up. It was my first real trophy, so you think I would be excited about it. But I just kept looking at Venus's trophy and wishing I could have somehow beaten her. Oh my God, I wanted that trophy so badly. Venus could see I was upset. After all, she was my big sister. She was used to taking care of me. She knew just what to do to pick me up. She came up to me after the awards ceremony and said: "You know what, Serena? I've been thinking. I've always liked silver better than gold. You want to trade?" ' Serena, winner of 12 grand slam singles titles, said: 'It's the most meaningful trophy I have ever received.'

The sisters then embarked on a life where they were often in each other's company. Richard tried to keep his daughters playing in separate tournaments but both had to play in the major ones. They travelled together, lived together. Indeed, their first mansion in Florida was shared. They bought the property in 2000 for $2.7m. It was near the family home. Serena bought a luxury multi-million dollar flat in California two years later. But the sisters are happy living together. They can share breakfast in a rented house in London in the morning before trading blows in the final of Wimbledon in the afternoon.

But the sisters are more comfortable cheering each other on than playing against each other. They have highly-tuned competitive instincts that are slightly blunted when facing each other. They watch each other play with a great anxiety. When Venus was struggling against Martina Hingis in the semi-final of the 1999 US Open, Serena had been watching the match in the locker room. But when Venus lost another game, she jumped up and strode to the courtside, saying: 'She needs me.'

There have been claims that the sisters do not give their all against each other. Some say that Richard decides who wins. But could a loving father tell a daughter to lose a grand slam final? Both sisters have rubbished the claims. 'It's absurd,' says Serena. 'It's enraging. I bristle every time I hear that. But what can you do? People are going to say what they want to say and believe what they want to be believe.'

Venus admits it is hard playing her sister. But

not for the reason everyone assumes. It is not just about playing a member of the family across the net. It is also about facing an opponent who is the most powerful hitter in women's tennis.

Venus says: 'I am serving at 125mph and the ball comes back at my feet faster.' She adds: 'When we step on to the court for sure we are not going to give each other a point but when we step off the court we'll say: "Geez, you should have played better" or "Wow, you played well. I could not get a point off you".'

There are always warm embraces at the end of matches. And Venus says: 'I don't hold it against any of my opponents if they beat me. So why should I with Serena? She is my flesh and blood. I think most people should see it in that way. That's the way it should be. A lot of people don't. They think we should fight. But we do not.'

The deluded criticisms over 'fixed matches' never bother Venus. 'I mean, if I thought everybody else was right, I probably would not have left Compton. I do not get too caught up in what the next person thinks.'

The Williams sisters walk their own way. But there is always a helping hand along the way. Venus and Serena talk every day, whether on the phone or in person. They have different interests and commercial concerns away from court but they shop together and stay together when at big tournaments. There is never any doubt that they are close.

When Serena had her meltdown at the US Open in 2009, Venus watched it from the stands. The sisters could not avoid the press in the aftermath of the row when Serena bad-mouthed an official. They had a doubles final to play on the same court that had witnessed Serena's rant just two days earlier. They won it, of course. It was their tenth grand slam title as a doubles partnership. They were presented with their trophy on court and had to face questions from Patrick McEnroe, brother of John. The television commentator brought up the controversy over Serena swearing. 'I'd like to thank the fans for supporting me through everything,' said Serena.

There was applause among the thousands in the Arthur Ashe stadium. 'I really, really love you guys and never want to have a bad image for you guys,' she added. McEnroe pushed further, trying to ask follow-up questions. The crowd started booing. Venus, the big sister, stepped in. 'I think what the crowd is saying is, "Patrick, let's move on",' Venus said.

The sisters still had to face the journalists in the press room. Serena was bombarded with questions. But Venus was at her side. She bristled at one persistent reporter: 'Are you trying to get aggressive on me?' It was a difficult situation. Serena was facing a media who were demanding that she should make a bigger apology to the lineswoman and to the sport.

It could have been a disaster for the sisters. But together they survived. Serena had been the target, but Venus had been the protector. It was the role she has always played. Yet there was one sister she could not save. No one could. The tragedy of Yetunde makes the tennis rows seem small and meaningless.

The Williams Sisters

11.

Yetunde Hawanya Tara Price

(Born August 9, 1972. Died: September 14, 2003)

> **She's gone.**
> A cousin's message to Serena

PHONE CALLS at 4am rarely herald good news. The ringing of the phone in the early hours of a Toronto morning disturbed Serena. She was in the Canadian city after winning an acting role in a television series. Injured and with time to spare, she was dedicating her attentions to acting. It is a career that she hopes to pursue after tennis. The call was from her mother, Oracene. It was a strange conversation. Oracene wanted to know if Serena had heard from her big sister, Yetunde. 'I can't reach her,' said Oracene. 'I think maybe something has happened. Maybe she has been involved in a car accident, or a shooting.'

Serena, who had been sleeping, was fully awake now. She phoned Yetunde's home. One of her cousins answered the phone. 'That's when I heard she had been involved in an accident. That she had been shot,' said Serena. The cousin said: 'She's gone, Serena. I am so sorry.' The joyous, successful life of the Williams family had been shattered by gunfire.

The reason that Oracene had phoned Serena was because someone had told her Yetunde had been injured. It was the call made by someone who wanted to alert the Williams family but not reveal the whole, terrible truth. Yetunde, aged just 31, had died back in Compton. The ghetto had made one last deadly call to her. Her life ended on the night of September 14, 2003. She was shot in the head while riding in an SUV driven by a friend, Rolland Wormley, believed to be the intended victim.

Southside Crips gang member Robert Edward Maxfield, 25, pleaded no contest to voluntary manslaughter on March 22, 2006, the day before his third trial in the killing was scheduled to start. The first trial ended in a mistrial. In the second trial, the jury could not come to a decision. Maxfield was sentenced to 15 years in prison.

But why was the sister of multi-millionaire sisters sitting in a vehicle outside a house known as a gang venue in the middle of one of the most dangerous areas in California, if not the USA? Wormley had driven her there. There were reports there had been an argument between Wormley and others outside the vehicle. Shots rang out. Yetunde's life was ended in the ghetto she thought she had escaped. 'Just like that she was gone,' said Serena.

Yetunde had stayed in California when the family moved to Florida. She was older and did not want to go from one side of the country to another. Yetunde was also involved in successive relationships with men in Compton. At the time of the family move, Yetunde was training as a nurse. She was also about to have her first child. The father was Jeffrey Johnson, a member of the Bloods gang. Johnson was later arrested for assaulting a police officer. Yetunde then met and married Byron Bobbitt, who had a criminal record for drugs and firearms offences.

Yetunde seemed to be drawn to dangerous company. She was proud, too. She would not take money from the sisters. Even when she worked as personal assistant to Serena, Yetunde insisted on paying her own fare to foreign tournaments. But she wanted her own life. And she worked hard to make it. She was a typical daughter of Richard and Oracene. She had her own mind. It was not easily changed. After her nursing training she became a hairdresser, moving to the more upmarket Corona, 40 miles from Compton. Yetunde started a business with hairdressing and beauty treatments. It was going well. She was making money. She had three children: Jeffrey, Justus and Jair. Life seemed to be on the up. Then on that fateful night she went for a late dinner and a drive back to Compton with her boyfriend, Wormley.

Serena was close to Yetunde, the oldest of all the Williams sisters. She doted on her nephews and niece. The news hit her hard, almost broke her. 'It was a real dark period in my life. I went through depression. I never even talked about it to my mom. No one knew I was in therapy, but I was. I was so close to her,' she said.

Venus was in shock. Years later she said her faith had survived the loss of her sister. 'It was just fate,' she said sadly. 'It happens all the time, to so many people.' Venus was also asked if she felt guilty, if she felt she should have given Yetunde money to move on to another life.

'You know what, I don't feel guilty,' she said. 'It would be pointless to feel that. I am less judgmental now, I think. I think of her every day, I try to remember her laughing.' Venus took nine months off from the game to mourn.

Isha, now the oldest sister, said of the pain of grief: 'I'm not sure it ever goes away – there's a part of me in the pit of my stomach that always falls, whenever something reminds me of her.'

Serena told the judge at the sentencing of Yetunde's killer: 'Our family has always been positive and we always try to help people.' She said later: 'I was just saying that we've always tried to be a positive role model for people that come from a ghetto. You can make something out of your life. You can start at zero and come out and have something. It's not about having money, it's about having pride and about upping your community. You see so many inspirational black people, but who do these people look up to? The rappers? Who, granted, are great people, I don't have anything against rappers, but some of the role models that African-Americans have aren't the best role models.'

Serena had looked up to her sister. Yetunde was bright and generous. She bought Serena clothes to go back to school out of the money she earned in a shop. She protected both Venus and Serena when boys made catcalls as they practised at the public courts as kids. But Yetunde was dead. Life had to go on. The biggest problem was the fight for the future of Yetunde's three children.

'My mom took the lead on this one,' said Serena. Oracene moved into Yetunde's home and started to look after the children. The children had two different fathers. One decided that it was better for the youngsters to lead their life with Oracene. They would have much more opportunity being brought up by a family with money and property. The other father resisted. He was Byron Bobbitt, who was divorced by Yetunde a year before she died. But Oracene pressed on. She finally won the battle. Her grandchildren are now in her care.

Serena and Venus eventually returned to the tennis courts. But they were damaged. Serena felt the loss keenly. She said of her oldest sister: 'She was gone, and the four of us would have to take in turns in her number one spot, filling the spaces where she had been.' But there was a gap in all their lives. Serena found it hard to fill.

12. Serena: the hidden struggle

*People see me on the court only as a
superhero, grunting and winning.
They think you're a robot and I'm not.*
                                        Serena

THE WORDS are emblazoned across a
formidable frontage. Are You Looking at My
Titles? shouts the tight Nike T-shirt. Serena sits
and smiles. Buxom and beautiful, Serena is aware
of the naughty side of the message. But the incident
seems to sum up the contradictions of Serena.
Deeply religious, she has no problem playing on
her sexiness. But the apparent confidence hides
some insecurity. The T-shirt was won in the
immediate aftermath of Wimbledon 2009. Serena
had just beaten her sister to record an astonishing
eleven grand slam singles titles.

But it has not been a trouble-free career. Serena
has endured much. Serena won just one major
tournament in the four years immediately after
Yetunde was killed. Chris Evert, the all-time great
women's tennis player, wrote an open letter to
Serena in Tennis magazine in 2006. She told Serena
she could be the greatest woman player and she
was betraying her talent. Serena was dismissive. 'I

thought she was entitled to her opinion,' Serena says. 'Before, I didn't really talk about other people, and since then I've done it less, because you don't know what's going on behind closed doors.'

What was going on behind closed doors with Serena? There were the physical problems. Serena needed surgery for a chronic knee injury. Her weight seemed to be rising amid reports of over-eating. She is a big woman, and she seemed to be getting bigger. Her emotional state was fragile, too. 'It was a very difficult time in my life. I still get teary-eyed talking about it,' she says. 'I didn't leave my house for weeks. I didn't talk to anybody. It was hard on my sisters, because when you're used to talking to somebody every day and you just don't talk to them, and they want to help you but you don't want to accept help. . . It's not easy.'

Serena came back. It is what she does.

She was a fighter as a four-year-old on the court in Compton. She is a fighter as a multi-millionaire. Her personality is hardly simple. 'I'm a real extrovert,' she says, 'but when I'm round someone new, I'm super shy. Actually, I'm lying. The older I get, the more extroverted I get. I'm super extroverted.'

She is also complicated. Her life is marked by her successes on court. But it is shaped by her family relationships. Serena admits she was always the spoiled child. 'I was the princess. I was everybody's pet,' she says.

She kept her eyes on Venus. Serena believed, maybe still does, that Venus summed up everything that was good in life. Venus was pretty, confident and successful as a child. Serena was desperate to be the same. The younger sister was immediately a relentless competitor. She cheated when playing against Venus. She cheated, too, when playing once against a tough opponent as a child. She is ashamed about that but knows it revealed how much she wanted to win. She was merciless in tournaments, winning 46 out of the 49 she contested in the under-10 age group in California. Yetunde, watching from the sidelines, would say: 'You beat that girl like she stole something. What did she steal of yours?'

Serena has risen to become one of the greatest players the game has ever seen. But there are flaws behind the confident smile. Serena claims to love looking in the mirror but has problems with her self-image. How can this be so? Surely, her array of daring outfits speak of a woman at peace with herself? Serena has worn denim mini-skirts on court. She has sprayed on a catsuit and prowled with menace in the US Open. She has even worn sexy boots as she has walked to take her seat in major tournaments. But she can be fragile. She said after her break-up to an American football player she does not wish to name: 'He left me thinking I was ugly, that I did not deserve to be in a loving relationship. Heck, I didn't love me anymore.' That self-love has been restored over the years.

Serena has found purpose and happiness outside of tennis. She is heavily involved in charity work. She started schools in Senegal and Nigeria. 'You make meaningful changes with small strokes,' she says. Serena believes the most important part of education is that it gives people a chance. 'You need to be strong,' she says, 'but you also need a shot. Strength is nothing without an opportunity to put it to use.'

She visited the 'slave castles' in Ghana. This is where the African slaves were held until they were taken on their awful voyages to a life in shackles in the USA. 'How could you not cry over something like this?' she says. 'How can you not be changed?' Serena's problems were put into some sort of perspective. 'My mindset changed as a result of that trip,' she says of her journey to Africa.

Serena also made time to start a fashion business. She designs many of the clothes she wears. She also pursues an acting career. Serena has been in a variety of TV and film roles. Most notably, she was a teacher in My Wife and Kids, a TV comedy. She also made fleeting appearances in the Black Knight and Beauty Shop, starring Queen Latifah. She enjoys reading, particularly Maya Angelou, and loves her dogs, a Jack Russell terrier and a Maltese terrier.

Her love life has been splattered over magazines and newspapers since she broke through to the top.

Serena has been linked with basketball players, American football players and even Brett Ratner, the director of Rush Hour, the highly successful film. In 2009, she admitted to dating the rapper Common. She has certain rules over relationships that meet with life as a Jehovah's Witness. 'I don't live with people unless I'm married,' she says. 'We don't believe in dating unless you're ready to get married. I've never dated anybody. It's good to get experience under your belt but you should never get wild or go crazy. If I can't see myself with this person for life – I can't be bothered. I can't waste my time. I have some really good men friends but I believe in no sex before marriage. No fornicating. Stuff like that. I really believe in that. I mean, I'm not perfect. It's hard to live by the Bible standards but I'm really comfortable with me.' Her ideal man must be intelligent. 'A man who can think for himself, has his own mind, and has a lot of self-confidence.'

She had a big decision to make in the crisis after the death of Yetunde. Did she want to go on playing tennis? 'All my life I'd woken up to tennis, tennis, tennis. Even if I don't go to practise, I'm thinking about it all day. And to have it on your mind for 24 years is a long time. So that's what I was questioning. Is this something I really love. Is it something my dad wanted me to do? Is it something I'm doing 'cos Venus is doing it?'

She recalls that she has always felt she was

following in the footsteps of Venus. As a child, she was always told to order first when entering a restaurant. Otherwise, she would just have what Venus had. She was overshadowed by Venus as a young player. Venus was going to be the bigger star, everyone agreed. Except Richard. Daddy said that Serena would be the stronger and better player. And so it has proved. Venus has been brilliant but stands in the shade of her younger sister in terms of achievements on court. Serena came back from the horror of Yetunde's death and won two Wimbledons, three Australian Opens and a US Open.

In the 2007 final of the Australian Open, she faced the rising star in Maria Sharapova. Serena had been unseeded in the tournament. This means she faced a tough route to the final, playing better-ranked players all the way. But she was mentally and physically strong. 'I will not be denied' was her motto for the tournament. She demolished the Russian in the fierce heat of Melbourne. When the dust settled on the astonishing victory, Serena accepted the trophy and turned to the crowd. She gave a victory speech from the bottom of her heart. 'Most of all I would like to dedicate this victory to my sister who is not here. Her name is Yetunde, and I just love her so much.'

13. Venus: Below the Surface

She has an old soul.
Sister Isha on Venus

VENUS sits in a side room at Wimbledon. She is giving a news conference exclusively to the British press. Two hours before stepping into this cramped space Venus beat her sister in the Wimbledon final of 2008. As the journalists grab chairs and gather round her, Venus takes her ease. Dressed in a fashionable mini skirt, her long legs stretch towards the reporters. Her legs start in Wimbledon SW19. They seem to end in SW20. She is glamorous, charming and funny. But she reveals nothing.

'She is ditsy,' says one journalist later. He compares Venus to a dumb blonde. He is wrong. Venus has two ways of dealing with the press. She can be sweet. She can also be aggressive when she feels the question is unfair or unjust. But they both amount to one thing. Venus only tells the world what she wants the world to know. And most times that is not much. Venus is very, very smart.

She has managed to keep a degree of privacy

despite being a superstar. She has managed to keep her fortune growing through ten years in tennis. She has expanded her life. She has continued to learn. And she has prepared for life after tennis. There are depths to Venus. She is not a one-dimensional sportswoman.

'Tennis does not define me,' she says. 'My parents taught me to be really well-rounded and to be more than just an athlete.' Yet she was intensely focused as a rising star. 'I don't remember learning how to play. I remember always knowing how to play,' she says.

Venus has suffered three great crises in her tennis career. She has survived all of them. The little girl of four who battered 500 balls during a training session with her father was always destined to be the best in the world. And Venus has reached the No.1 spot. But she has been eclipsed in achievements by her younger sister. There is evidence that this hurt.

After Venus lost the semi-finals of the US Open in 1999, she had to watch her sister win the tournament. Serena had won the first grand slam singles title for the Williams family. It was not supposed to be like that and Oracene talked of the pain that Venus was feeling. 'I told her everything would be fine. But she did not want to hear that,' says Oracene. She later added: 'Maybe this is a wake-up call for Venus. To be tougher. This will be an example. Venus has the ability that no one has seen yet: it would be impossible to even describe it.'

Venus, it seemed, had to add a mental toughness. She did just this as she moved on from crisis No.1. Despite reports of her considering an early retirement, Venus battled though serious wrist injuries and won grand slams the next year. Serena has over the years won more major titles than Venus. But big sister has still seized seven grand slam titles. It is a highly impressive achievement and puts her among the best women tennis players ever.

She is also one of the most intriguing. Venus has always had a life beyond the court. As a young girl, she read a lot and was interested in learning outside the classroom, too. Although juggling a growing tennis career with school life, Venus always attained excellent marks. Richard says: 'Venus reached my expectations when she went to Morningside High School in Inglewood, California. She made As in mathematics, in trigonometry, and set a record that stood for a long time. I pushed education. I wanted them to understand that you can be the greatest athlete in the world but without the greatest knowledge in the world, you are going to lose all your money anyway.'

Venus was already a multi-millionaire when she graduated from high school. But this did not stop her wanting to learn. She later graduated from the Art Institute of Fort Lauderdale and studied interior design at a college in Palm Beach. Venus was doing all this when trying to be the best player in the world. She did most of the work as the tennis season wound down through October, November and December and completed many assignments online. But she never gave up. She was motivated. She even encouraged Serena to further her education. 'Serena and I have gone to college for the same reason that everyone else does – so we have more options in life,' she says. 'There is life after tennis and we don't plan to be sitting on the sidelines.'

Venus has made tens of millions of dollars from endorsements from such as Nike and McDonalds. She has earned $25m in prize money on court. But she has also developed her own companies. She has her fashion label, EleVen, and an interior design company, VStarr Interiors. She works hard on court. She works hard off it, too.

'I don't have time or the desire to live what some people view as the excessive lifestyle of the rich and famous,' she says. 'I have always been smart with my money and I have professionals who help me make the right financial choices.'

But what is she like as a person? Most professionals in the dressing-room view her as cool and distant. Venus keeps to her own small circle.

She feels no need to disarm people with charm. 'I am not really intimidated by anyone. Why should I be?' she says. She even took on the President of the USA. When Bill Clinton phoned Venus after she won the US Open in 2000, Venus quizzed him on why he had left the final early. She also asked him if he could do anything to lower her taxes. But she is not immune to painful emotions. She suffered badly in the wake of the death of Yetunde. This was her second crisis and she emerged from it hurt but intact.

The third crisis has been a series of professional setbacks in recent years. These have been, of course, much less painful than her personal loss. 'I think everyone has moments of doubt but for me I think I know that I've put the time in on court or whatever I am pursuing. I'll just work and work and I'll just do it over and over and over again,' she says. 'And I know I have spent the time and I have confidence. Any time I try something new, I just work at it and that builds confidence. That's how I maintain my confidence.'

She adds: 'Challenges are not intimidating to me. Challenges motivate me and make me better. If I were intimidated by a challenge, I would not be where I am today.'

If this sounds like a severe young woman, there is a softness to Venus, too. Her friends talk of her generosity of spirit. Serena speaks of Venus as her protector, the perfect big sister. The woman dubbed the Ice Queen of Wimbledon also has a passionate side. She is in a long-term relationship with professional golfer Hank Kuehne. And she has interests far beyond tennis and commerce. She loves music and plays the guitar. Like Serena, she loves dogs and has a Yorkshire terrier. She is keen on languages and studies Spanish, Russian and French. She made a gracious speech in French after winning the French Open.

And she can be as sloppy and relaxed as most other people. She treats herself to a McDonalds when she feels she deserves a lift after a loss. She enjoys chilling out in front of the television. One favourite programme is the Golden Girls. No, not a biography of Venus and her sister, but a comedy on the lives of three older women.

She is still focused on tennis, however. 'I put tennis at the forefront of everything,' she says. 'If I think other things are a distraction to tennis, I take a step back from those other things.' She will, of course, have to take a step back from tennis. Already plagued with injuries, particularly to her knees, another life beckons. Venus is prepared for it. It will be fascinating to watch just what she does. 'I don't like mainstream. I want to be ahead of the curve,' she says. 'I don't like to be the same as every-body else.'

14. Faith, Hope and Charity

You can do all things no matter
what obstacles are thrown in your way.
Venus Williams

THE WILLIAMS sisters are different. And not just because of their success, their millions of dollars, or their background as African-Americans from a ghetto upbringing triumphing in a middle-class sport. Another aspect separates the Williams from their fellow competitors, even their fans. Both Venus and Serena are Jehovah's Witnesses. They were brought up in that religion by their mother and father.

So who are Jehovah's Witnesses, and what do they believe? The religion has attracted controversy, but what religion has not? There are more than six million members worldwide. The name comes from the book of Isaiah in the Old Testament where the world is portrayed as a scene from a courtroom drama. The witnesses to the truth are the followers of Jehovah [God].

Jehovah's Witnesses are, of course, famous for going from door to door to spread their faith. Both Serena and Venus have done this, though understandably it has become more difficult over the years. 'I want to knock on people's doors and preach. But I also meet a lot of people on planes and in restaurants, and you can preach with them or place some literature with them,' says Serena.

Jehovah's Witnesses believe in an Armageddon that will end the world. Only the righteous will be risen up from the dead. Famously, they refuse to accept blood transfusions. They do not celebrate Christmas, believing it to derive from a pagan tradition. They also refuse to be involved in politics, though Venus once questioned the then President of the United States on her taxes when she received his call after she won the US Open. They believe all sexual relationships outside of marriage are grounds for expulsion (known as 'disfellow-shipping'). They also advocate modesty in dress. No-one quite knows what the leaders of the religion make of the Williams sisters' skimpy on-court costumes.

But no one can deny the sincerity of their faith. It breathes hope into their lives. It brings their charity into the lives of others. Both sisters devote time, energy and money to building schools in Africa, to supporting cancer charities and to helping under-privileged children. Their business lives, including the purchase of the National Football League team, the Miami Dolphins, attract big headlines. But the Williams – mother, father and daughters – all testify to the need to be charitable.

That is, after all, part of their faith.

This was tested by the shooting of Yetunde. Serena, in particular, retreated into herself, cutting herself off from the outside world. 'When you don't go to your Christian meetings, it takes its toll,' she said of a time when she was laid low by grief. 'I wasn't going because I never left my house and instead of taking comfort in what I should have done, which is reading Bible scriptures, I didn't. But I learned that I could help others to say this isn't the right way. How do I know? Because I've experienced it.'

She believes totally. She said of her religion: 'We're dealing with serious concerns like what is the world coming to? Everything is going downhill in terms of the economy, and the green stuff. What's going to happen to this world? In the Bible it talks about how God's going to restore the world to a paradise, and God is someone who keeps his promises. Jehovah says he would never destroy this world, so if you believe in the Bible, those things are comforting to know.'

Serena also revealed in her autobiography how she prayed fervently when she was at the centre of the storm at the Indian Wells tournament. Constantly abused by fans in the final, she just asked for the strength to come through the ordeal. And she did. In an article for the evangelical magazine Guideposts in October 2004, she wrote about the power of prayer. 'It is as sure as my two-handed backhand,' she wrote. 'One rule in tennis is that every other game you switch ends of the court with your opponent. Every changeover, I bow my head, close my eyes. And I pray: Help me stay strong out here. Help me stay calm and do my best. Thank you, Lord.'

Her sister is just as devoted. 'It's made a huge difference in my life,' Venus says. 'All the girls I grew up with had hardships that they were not able to get through but I think having a solid family and solid religious beliefs helped me and my sister find that stability. And even if life was going crazy on court and even if I had a horrible year and even if I was mad and could not get off the couch because I was playing so bad I didn't even want to go to practise, well, you know, I felt that was not the most important thing and my life was not going to end.'

She has a message for all young people striving to make their way in life. 'I want them to know that you can do all things no matter what obstacles are thrown in your way. Challenge those obstacles and overcome the situation,' she says.

Both sisters regularly attend Kingdom Hall, the meeting place for Jehovah's Witnesses. They discuss the Bible there and believe most of it is literally true. They have been the subject of criticism, even ridicule, for their faith. But they are used to facing opposition. They have always had to contend with racism, sometimes subtle, sometimes brutally crude. Their mother helped them find a way through it with her belief in a higher power. 'It's like the Bible says. If someone is talking bad about you, be happy. I schooled the girls on the n-word issue. I said you might get called that and if you do just say: "Thank you. I love it". Eventually when they see it doesn't bother you, they leave it alone,' says Oracene.

The Williams sisters have found themselves in the midst of storms. Some of these have been as silly as feuds with other players. Some have been as ugly as the booing from crowds. Others have been genuinely tragic, such as the death of their sister. But they have always come through. They will testify that they have been helped by their faith in God. But belief, in turn, has helped them in another type of faith that sustains them, even propels them to further success. The Williams sisters believe in God. But they believe in themselves, too.

Afterword

PAT, PAT, PAT, PAT. The grand slam champion bounces the ball on the hardcourt in Melbourne, Australia. The ball flies into the air and the service action is unleashed. A cry of 'foot fault' breaks the silence at the Rod Laver Arena.

'Did you just foot-fault me in a charity match? You're kidding me, right?' The voice is that of Andy Roddick, the American who won his country's Open championship in 2003. It is January 2010 and he is playing in a match in aid of the victims of the Haitian earthquake disaster. He takes the foot fault in his stride. He tells the lineswoman: 'You realise Serena is sitting over there.'

Serena is, indeed, at courtside. And she tilts her head and laughs. It is the first major tournament after the furore of Flushing Meadows. The huge fine on Serena still stings. It's not about the money. But the Williams camp feels that an example is being made when others have escaped such severe punishment. Serena, too, is suffering from being placed under probation. If she commits another major offence, she will miss the US Open.

Serena is contrite, yet again. 'I felt incredibly bad and miserable for losing my cool, and most importantly not representing the person I really am spiritually and the role model I want to be to my young fans,' she says in Melbourne. 'I have been a feisty player all my life but when the time came for me to be calm and cool I did not exercise a mild temper. I apologised to my fans and even wrote a personal letter to the lineswoman with my apologies. She was extremely supportive and said that she did not think any further action should be taken against me.'

She reveals the depth of her resentment when she tells a television station: '$92,000 is a lot of money to fine someone. I always said what I did wasn't right, but I turned that around and I'm actually raising $92,000 to educate ladies, women, also for my school in Africa. Also I'm giving some money to Haiti, as well. So, you know, I don't know whoever got fined like that. People said worse, done worse. I just thought it was a bit . . . I think it was a bit much.'

If Serena is nursing a sense of grievance, she is also nursing a series of aches and pains. One writer remarks as a heavily-bandaged Serena comes on court for the first round: 'Here comes mummy. An Egyptian mummy.' The chemists in Melbourne must have been stripped of bandages. Serena is strapped from head to toe.

After the tournament, Serena patiently goes through the reasons for each bandage. 'I pulled a hamstring in Sydney, so I was devastated by that. However, when I strapped it, it felt a lot better. And then something happened to the side of my leg in Sydney. And then when I strapped it, it didn't feel better, but it helped a little bit. And, of course, I tape my ankles for prevention. In the third round I twisted my ankle, and then I fell and hurt my wrist. And then somewhere in between there my toes started hurting so they had to be taped.'

All the pain, though, was accompanied by glory. 'I don't know any athlete who doesn't at any point play in pain,' Serena says. 'That's the thing about being an athlete, you go and you play. Two weeks of hard labour is rewarded with her 12th grand slam title. Serena beats Urszula Radwanska, Petra Kvitoza, Carlo Suarez Navorro, Samantha Stosur, Victoria Azarenko, Na Li and then Justine Henin, who has come back to tennis after retirement, in the final. The ignominy of defeat to a Belgian through default in the US Open is replaced by the joy of beating another Belgian in the very next grand slam final. Serena takes the title through her mixture of grit, talent, bloody-mindedness and strength. She simply refuses to be beaten. Azarenko runs her close. Henin poses questions. Serena answers them all.

The 6-4, 3-6, 6-2 win marks the 12th grand slam for Serena and the 5th singles title for the American in Melbourne. Serena has now tied with Billie-Jean King in grand slam titles won.

The tournament has been a redemption for Serena. Venus was defeated by Na Li, the Chinese player. But Serena took her revenge beating Li in straight sets. However, Venus is undaunted. She has not won a grand slam title since Wimbledon 2008 but she is not about to give up.

'As usual, I try to learn from my mistakes and move on. I mean, I don't hang on to things because there's lot more matches ahead,' she says sweetly in the aftermath of defeat. But the warrior spirit is still there. She is asked: 'What do you say to people that say Wimbledon or the US Open is your only hope of another major?'

Venus replies: 'I don't know. Are you saying that?'

Journalist: 'No.'

Venus: 'Just making sure.'

Almost inevitably, though, she shares in a grand slam doubles victory again with her sister, beating Cara Black and Liezel Huber in the final.

But as Venus nudges 30, with Serena only little more than a year behind, the questions turn with a weary predictability to how long they can dominate at the top of the sport. They have, after all, other lives to lead in fashion, design and charity work.

Serena insists she is still fresh. 'That's why I always do design and fashion, because right when I'm there [stale], you know, I take my little break. I make sure I have my schedule where I do have breaks and where I don't play certain tournaments. You know, I think it's important to just have a normal life because at the end of the day I'm not going to be playing till I'm a hundred.'

Venus is quieter, though insistent that she has still something to give. But it is difficult to see the older sister going on indefinitely if she cannot win grand slams. Venus exists to win the major tournaments, to make history. This was never really about money for her. With tens of millions of dollars at her back, it is certainly not about the cash now. She is aware that winning is not going to get any easier. A new generation is coming through. The Belgians, Kim Clijsters and Henin, have returned and shown immediately that they can compete at the very highest level.

The question of continuing in the sport is an easier one for the younger sister. Serena, when the mood moves her, can be invincible. And she shows no signs of wanting to quit. As she walks away with her 12th grand slam singles title, she is asked if she has given herself a timeline to continue in the game. 'Oh, God, no,' she says. There is the smallest of pauses before she adds: 'Yeah, I say till someone takes me out back and shoots me.'

The message is clear. There are more chapters to come in the Williams story.

Note on Sources

The Williams sisters have lived their lives illuminated by a media glare. Some of the writing about them holds little value but there is a mass of excellent work on the remarkable sisters.

I am greatly indebted to Jaqueline Edmondson's *Venus and Serena Williams: A Biography* (Greenwood Press, 2005) for opening up avenues to explore further.

L J Wertheim's *Venus Envy: A Sensational Season Inside the Women's Tennis Tour* (HarperCollins, 2001) was crucial in gauging the reaction, both adverse and positive, to the arrival of a remarkable talent.

Charging The Net: A History of Blacks in Tennis by Cecil Harris and Larryette Kyle-DeBose (Ivan R Dee, 2007) is a brilliant, moving and inspiring chronicle of black tennis that was invaluable to the chapters on the controversy at Indian Wells and the one on Arthur Ashe and Althea Gibson. Much of its sensibility permeates other chapters.

Venus & Serena by Mark Stewart (Millbrook Press, 2000) was also useful.

There were two major sources of interviews on the sisters. *Sports Illustrated's* website has an astonishing archive of material on the sisters. I am grateful for the information on matches and on interviews that are contained there.

ASAP, the company that records every interview at a major tennis tournament, also holds records of formal interviews with both sisters. This is a resource that is being constantly updated, allowing the reader and writer to chart the progress of the sisters.

Harpo, the producers of the Oprah Winfrey Show, also has interviews with both sisters and both parents.

The websites of both sisters were also useful.

Websites such as macleans.ca and cnn.com/asia also carried excellent interviews with Richard and Venus Williams respectively. Urbaninfluence.com revealed much of Venus's love of fashion and *Ebony* magazine has chronicled the sisters' rise to fame over the years.

Venus Williams has not yet written her biography but *My Life: Queen of the Court* by Serena Williams (Simon and Schuster, 2009) informs much of this book, particularly the tragedy of Yetunde.

Sources

Simon Hattenstone's subsequent interview with Serena in *The Guardian* provided a poignant portrait of a sister coming to terms with grief.